FROM SEA to SHINING SEA

MONTANA

JUDITH M. WILLIAMS

Consultants

MELISSA N. MATUSEVICH, PH.D.
Curriculum and Instruction Specialist
Blacksburg, Virginia

MILLA L. CUMMINS, M.L.I.S.
Director
Livingston-Park County Public Library
Livingston, Montana

CHILDREN'S PRESS®
A DIVISION OF SCHOLASTIC INC.

New York • Toronto • London • Auckland • Sydney • Mexico City
New Delhi • Hong Kong • Danbury, Connecticut

Montana is in the northwestern part of the United States. It is bordered by Idaho, Wyoming, North Dakota, South Dakota, and Canada.

Project Editor: Meredith DeSousa
Art Director: Marie O'Neill
Photo Researcher: Marybeth Kavanagh
Design: Robin West, Ox and Company, Inc.
Page 6 map and recipe art: Susan Hunt Yule
All other maps: XNR Productions, Inc.

Library of Congress Cataloging-in-Publication Data

Williams, Judith M.
    Montana / by Judith M. Williams.
    p. cm. – (From sea to shining sea)
    Includes biographical references and index.
    Summary: Describes the geography, history, government, people, and places of
Montana.
    ISBN 0-516-22479-4
    1. Montana—Juvenile literature. [1. Montana.] I. Title. II. From sea to shining sea
(Series)

F731.3 .W55 2001
978.6—dc21   2001028913

TABLE of CONTENTS

CHAPTER

CHAPTER ONE

INTRODUCING THE TREASURE STATE

One of Montana's nicknames, "Big Sky Country," was inspired by scenes such as this one. The Bitterroot Mountains are in the background.

Montana is huge. Only Alaska, Texas, and California are larger. All the New England states (Maine, Vermont, New Hampshire, Massachusetts, Connecticut, and Rhode Island), plus New York and New Jersey would easily fit inside Montana, with room left over for half of Pennsylvania!

Despite Montana's large size, the state's population is surprisingly small. About nine hundred thousand people live there. So although Montana is 120 times larger in size than the tiny state of Rhode Island, it has almost 150,000 fewer people.

Montana is known as the Treasure State, and its treasures are many. Montana's natural resources—gold, copper, platinum, timber, coal, petroleum, and natural gas—enrich the state's economy. Its stunning landscape of rugged mountains, crystal blue skies, and endless plains provides a wealth of natural beauty. Finally, Montana's treasure chest holds a rich heritage of native peoples, mountain men, cattle drives, and pioneers.

What comes to mind when you think of Montana?

* Dinosaurs roaming the land millions of years ago
* Lewis and Clark exploring the great Missouri River
* Cattle drives on the open range
* Homesteaders breaking sod on the prairies
* American Indians defending their land
* Ghost towns that once thrived with mining activity
* Locomotives chugging across the wide-open plains
* Towering mountains and lush forests
* Abundant wildlife

Montana has grizzly bears, elk, and bighorn sheep. It has powwows, rodeos, and state fairs. Montana is Big Sky Country, where miles of open plains meet cloudless skies. In this book, you'll learn about the land, people, and events that made the Treasure State what it is today.

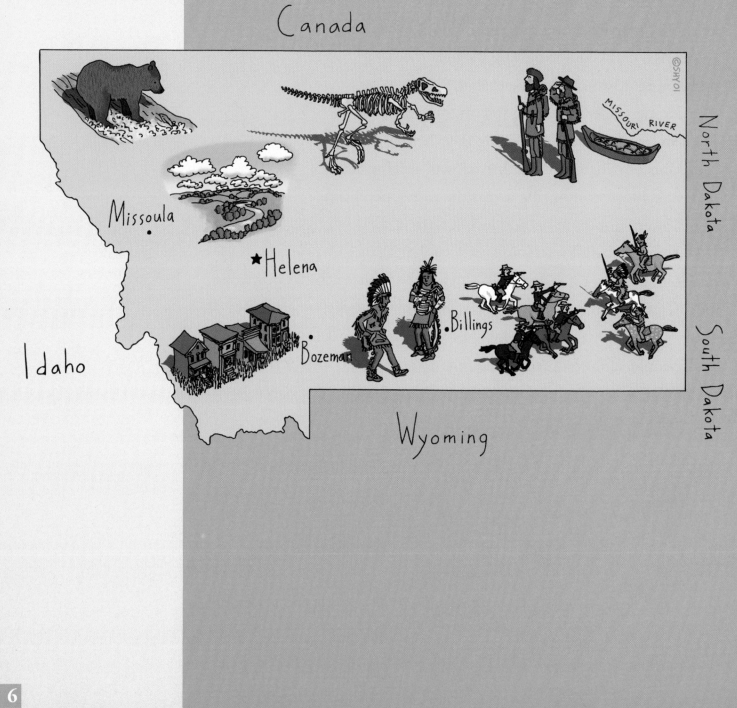

Canada

Idaho

Wyoming

North Dakota

South Dakota

Missoula

★Helena

Bozeman

.Billings

MISSOURI RIVER

©SHYOI

CHAPTER TWO

THE LAND OF MONTANA

Montana is in the northwestern region of the United States. Four states border Montana. North Dakota and South Dakota share the eastern border. Wyoming lies to the south, and Idaho curves around from the south to the northwest corner. Directly north of Montana lies another country, Canada. Montana is the only state to border three different Canadian provinces, or territories—British Columbia, Alberta, and Saskatchewan.

If you locate Montana on a map, you'll see it is almost rectangular in shape. The greatest distance from east to west is 545 miles (877 kilometers). The greatest distance north to south is 321 miles (517 km). In total, Montana covers 147,046 square miles (380,849 square kilometers). Of that area, only 1,490 square miles (3,859 sq km) is inland water.

Montana is one of six Rocky Mountain states, including Idaho, Wyoming, Colorado, Utah, and Nevada. The Rocky Mountains are the

Montana is a mix of expansive landscapes and impressive mountains.

7

largest mountain system in North America, and part of the mountain range runs through each of these six states. Like these other states, Montana is home to spectacular scenery and a western, outdoor style of life.

GEOGRAPHIC REGIONS

There are two major land regions in Montana. The Rockies run through the western part of the state to create the Rocky Mountain region. The rest of the state is in a region called the Great Plains.

The Rocky Mountains

The western part of Montana is made up of high mountain peaks, lush evergreen forests, low grassy valleys, and sparkling rivers. The Rocky Mountain region has more than fifty different mountain ranges, including the Absaroka, Beartooth, Beaverhead, Big Belt, Bitterroot, Bridger, Cabinet, Crazy, Flathead, Gallatin, Lewis, Little Belt, Madison, Mission, and Tobacco Root. Snow covers some of the highest peaks for more than nine months each year. The highest peak in Montana is Granite Peak, stretching 12,799 feet (3,901 meters) into the sky. Peaks that reach higher than 10,000 feet (3,281 m) are Froze-to Death Mountain, Electric Peak, Mosquito Mountain, Ramshorn Mountain, and Lone Mountain.

Glacier National Park, high in the Rockies, is part of the Waterton-Glacier International Peace Park, located in both Montana and Canada. Montana is the only state that shares a national park with another country.

In Glacier National Park, Reynolds Creek cascades down the rocks, creating a picturesque scene.

Visitors to the Rocky Mountain region of Montana may encounter grizzly and black bears, mountain goats, elk, moose, mule deer, pronghorn antelope, and wolves. Bighorn sheep travel the craggy mountainsides, near where golden eagles build aeries, or nests. Smaller mammals that live in the Rockies include dam-building beavers, coyotes, pumas, lynx, bobcats, minks, pine martens, weasels, otters and pikas.

Part of the Continental Divide, also called the Great Divide, runs along the Rocky Mountains. The Continental Divide is the area that separates the streams and rivers of North America into those that flow west toward the Pacific Ocean and those that flow east toward the Atlantic Ocean and the Gulf of Mexico.

Great Plains

The Great Plains lie to the east of the Rockies. Most of the land in this region is flat or has low-rolling hills. The plains are crisscrossed by dozens of rivers and streams, which cut low-lying valleys into the land. There are some isolated, or "island" mountains, such as Sweetgrass, Judith, Bearpaws, and Little Rocky. These island mountains jut up from

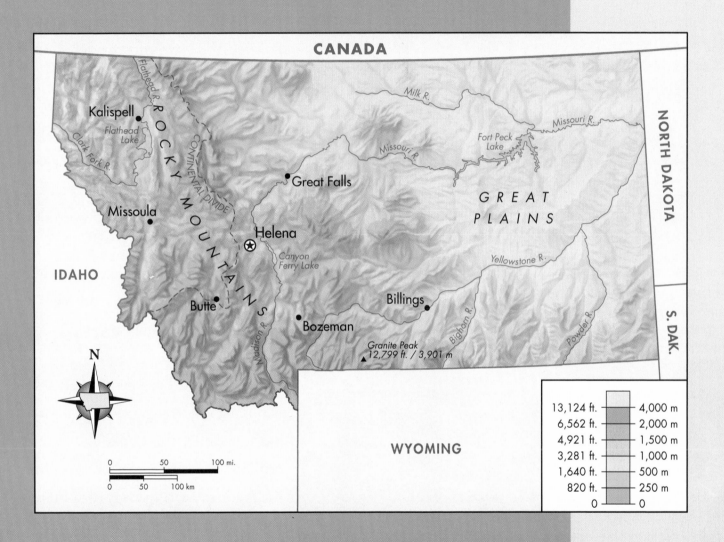

CANADA

NORTH DAKOTA

S. DAK.

IDAHO

WYOMING

Kalispell

Flathead Lake

Clark Fork R.

Flathead R.

ROCKY MOUNTAINS

CONTINENTAL DIVIDE

Missoula

Great Falls

Helena

Canyon Ferry Lake

Butte

Madison R.

Bozeman

Granite Peak
12,799 ft. / 3,901 m

Milk R.

Missouri R.

Missouri R.

Fort Peck Lake

GREAT PLAINS

Yellowstone R.

Billings

Bighorn R.

Powder R.

N

0   50   100 mi.

0   50   100 km

13,124 ft.	4,000 m
6,562 ft.	2,000 m
4,921 ft.	1,500 m
3,281 ft.	1,000 m
1,640 ft.	500 m
820 ft.	250 m
0	0

Pronghorn antelope are the fastest animals in North America—they can run at speeds of up to 70 miles (113 km) per hour.

the plains, rising to meet the clear blue sky.

The prairie is traditionally grass covered. The two most widely seen grasses are bluebunch wheatgrass and blue grama. Willows and cottonwood trees are commonly found in the Great Plains valleys. Daisies, Indian paintbrush, black-eyed Susans, and poppies sprinkle color across the plains.

Wild ducks, geese, and whooping cranes summer in the wetlands. Deer and pronghorn antelope are the largest animals to live on Montana's plains. Prairie dogs, black-footed ferrets, burrowing owls, and grouse also make their homes here.

In the southeastern corner of Montana is a strange geological formation called the badlands. Over millions of years, water erosion, or the gradual wearing away of land by water, formed this region of steep hills and deep ditches. Valleys and canyons are carved deep into the rock, making the badlands look like the surface of the moon.

EXTRA! EXTRA!

The prairie dog is what is known as a keystone species. Many other animals on the Montana prairie depend on the prairie dog for their own existence. Prairie dogs live in burrows, which are holes and tunnels under the ground. As they dig burrows they turn over the soil, keeping alive the grasses that feed bison and antelope. The burrows also provide shelter for voles and ground squirrels. Prairie dogs themselves serve as prey for coyotes, badgers, weasels, black-footed ferrets, and rattlesnakes.

The towering red cliffs of the Terry Badlands are located in Eastern Montana.

RIVERS AND LAKES

Montana is the only state that has river systems flowing in three different directions—east to the Atlantic Ocean (by way of the Gulf of Mexico), west to the Pacific Ocean, and north to Hudson Bay (in Canada). The Continental Divide winds through the state and separates the rivers flowing east and west.

The two most important rivers in Montana are the Missouri River and the Yellowstone River. The Missouri River begins in southwestern Montana where the Gallatin, Jefferson, and Madison Rivers meet. From there, the Missouri flows 2,315 miles (3,725 km) in an eastward direc-

This photograph shows the Marias River where it joins the Missouri River.

FIND OUT MORE

Look at a topographical map of the United States. Follow the Missouri River from its source to where it meets the Mississippi River. Through which states does the Missouri River pass? What other rivers flow into the Missouri River?

tion toward the Mississippi River. The Missouri's tributaries in Montana include the Marias, Milk, Sun, and Teton Rivers.

The Yellowstone River flows east and slightly north across the state from Yellowstone National Park, on the border of Montana and Wyoming. The Yellowstone River is the longest free-flowing river in the continental United States. It played an important role in the early exploration of this area by Meriwether Lewis and William Clark, who traveled along the river to explore many parts of the western United States. The main branches of the Yellowstone are the Bighorn, Clarks Fork, Powder, Stillwater, and Tongue Rivers.

Montana's rivers fall into two categories: Rocky Mountain rivers and plains rivers. The Flathead, Red Rock, Big Hole, Gallatin, Yellowstone, Jefferson, and Madison Rivers begin high in the Rockies. In spring, melting snow feeds these rivers. Plains rivers flow from west to east across the broad, flat plains. These include the Big Horn, Tongue, Powder, Milk, Musselshell, and Missouri Rivers.

Montana has hundreds of natural and manmade lakes. Flathead Lake, in northwestern Montana, is the largest natural lake in the state and the largest freshwater lake west of the Mississippi. It covers about 195 square

miles (505 sq km). Montana's artificial lakes, or reservoirs, were created by dams. The dams hold water and then periodically release it. The water is used to make hydroelectric power, or electricity. Generators and giant water wheels called turbines change the mechanical energy of flowing water into electrical energy that the people of Montana can use. The largest artificial lake is Fort Peck Lake on the Missouri River. Others include Canyon Ferry Lake, Hungry Horse, and Lake Koocanusa.

Montana's Flathead Lake is one of the largest—and the cleanest—natural lakes in the world.

FIND OUT MORE

The Hebgen Lake earthquake affected geysers in nearby Yellowstone Park. Geysers are eruptions of hot water from deep inside the earth. Normally, geysers erupt at predictable intervals, but the earthquake affected their eruption times. What causes a geyser to erupt?

CLIMATE

Montana's climate varies from one area to another because the state is so large and has such great differences in elevation. Summers are cooler and winters are warmer west of the Continental Divide. On average, summer temperatures in the west range from 79° to 85° Fahrenheit (26° to 29° Celsius), and in the east the average is 89°F (32°C). The average January temperature in the west is 20°F (–7°C), while in the east it is about 14°F (–10°C). Cold spells in the east are often broken by warm, dry winds called *chinooks*. Chinooks come down the eastern mountainsides to the plains and warm the land so that cattle can continue to graze even in winter.

Montana weather is known for its extremes. Major blizzards, hailstorms, and droughts are a part of life Montana residents have learned to live with. Hailstorms in the summer can sometimes cause injuries, as well as crop and property damage.

Montana also has a surprisingly large number of earthquakes, mostly in the western part of the state. Although most quakes are not strong enough for people to notice, even the smallest tremors are recorded in geological laboratories.

Montana's strongest earthquake occurred on August 17, 1959 at Hebgen Lake. The sudden movement of earth beneath the lake triggered a landslide in Madison River Canyon. The landslide created a dam on the Madison River, which resulted in the formation of a lake known as Quake Lake. Many homes and highways in the lake area were badly damaged, and at least twenty-eight people died.

CHAPTER THREE

MONTANA THROUGH HISTORY

Montana's first inhabitants, called Paleo-Indians, arrived about thirteen thousand years ago. They may have come to North America by traveling across a land bridge that stretched between present-day Russia and Alaska, settling in areas where food was plentiful. Two Paleo-Indian cultures lived in the area of present-day Montana—the Clovis Culture and the Folsom Culture. They lived on the plains and in the foothills of the mountains. They often moved from place to place, following the food supply. On foot, they hunted mammoths or prehistoric bison, killing them with stone spearheads.

About eight thousand years ago, descendants of the Paleo-Indians moved into the mountains, where clear streams were brimming with fish. They formed communities and lived in small groups. Native Americans gathered roots, berries, and nuts, and also fished and hunted elk, deer, and bison (sometimes called buffalo).

In the 1850s, Virginia City was a busy mining town.

17

FIND OUT MORE

After killing a bison, native people used all of its parts, often for things other than food. They ate the flesh, and tanned the hides to make tipis, clothing, and shoes. How were other parts of the bison used?

Native people relied on buffalo for most of their basic needs. Over time, they developed new methods of hunting buffalo. They drove the animals over steep cliffs. The buffalo plunged to their death, falling anywhere from 20 feet (6 meters) to 50 feet (15 m). This method of hunting buffalo became known as *pishkun.* Various Native American groups often banded together to carry out the hunt. Some groups traded buffalo meat in exchange for beans and other crops.

Eventually, Native Americans formed groups called tribes or clans. Tribes that had lived on the Great Plains of central North America began moving into the Montana region around A.D. 1600. Among the earliest tribes to hunt Montana's plains were the Shoshone and the Gros Ventre; the Blackfeet arrived later. The Plains Indians hunted bison, deer, and antelope, and fished the many rivers throughout the Great

Plains. They made homes from animal hides held up by wooden poles or animal bones. These homes could be taken down quickly. An entire tribe could be ready to move within a matter of hours.

The Bannock, Kalispel, Salish, and Kootenai lived in the mountains. They built villages, hunted and fished, and ate roots and berries. These tribes were called hunter-gatherers because they hunted and collected food instead of farming. Mountain natives built permanent homes called lodges. They used bark, hides, and branches from pine trees to keep out wind, rain, and snow.

When Spanish explorers arrived in parts of North America in the 1500s, the lives of Native Americans were forever changed. The Spanish brought horses from Europe, and within two hundred years, horses became the main form of transportation for many Native Americans. Their hunting became more efficient on horseback. Traveling and moving the tribe was easier. Mountain tribal hunters could travel far to the east in search of bison or deer. Plains Native Americans also hunted on horseback, using iron-tipped arrows to kill their prey.

ARRIVAL OF THE EUROPEANS

The earliest explorers to record their visit to present-day Montana were two Frenchmen, brothers François and Louis-Joseph de la Vérendrye. In 1743, they traveled through the southeastern corner of Montana in search of furs for their father's fur company. At this time, furs were in high demand in Europe. To Europeans, beaver hats were signs of wealth.

Native Americans became even more efficient at hunting buffalo after horses were introduced.

In general, the taller the beaver hat, the richer the person seemed. Fur was also used to trim coats and ladies' hats. Much money could be made from hunting and trapping animals to obtain their fur, which was then sold for a profit. After the brothers' visit, other French and Spanish hunters and trappers discovered the rich bounty of Montana's land and set up trading posts in the region.

Eventually, the French claimed most of the Great Plains region. In 1762, a treaty between the French and Spanish gave present-day Montana to Spain. In 1800, Spain returned the land to France. France now owned a large piece of North America that was known as the Louisiana Territory, which included a large portion of what is today Montana. In 1803, the United States bought the Louisiana Territory from France for $15 million.

FIND OUT MORE

The Louisiana Territory was so big that the United States doubled in size after making the purchase. How many states were once part of the Louisiana Territory?

THE LEWIS AND CLARK EXPEDITION

After the Louisiana Purchase, President Thomas Jefferson sent an expedition to explore the new territory. He wanted to know where fur trapping and trading would be most profitable. Captain Meriwether Lewis, Jefferson's secretary, and William Clark, an army lieutenant, shared command of the expedition.

In 1804, Lewis and Clark's Corps of Discovery set off from St. Louis, Missouri. The corps had 48 members, most of whom were army men. At Mandan Villages, a French Canadian named Toussaint Charbonneau joined the expedition, along with his fifteen-year-old Shoshone wife, Sacagawea, and their baby. Sacagawea was especially helpful to the expedition. She served as a guide in her Montana homeland and helped the corps to buy horses from the Shoshone nation. Also, her presence persuaded Native American groups that the expedition was not a war party.

Sacagawea is shown acting as an interpreter between Lewis and Clark and the Chinook.

The Corps of Discovery explored Montana, heading west along the Missouri River. Lewis and Clark made notes along the way, describing the plants, animals, and people they saw. They were amazed by the area's wildlife, including buffalo herds numbering as many as 10,000. They were the first Europeans to describe grizzly bears in writing. The expedition met with many native people along the way. Lewis described the Salish (Flathead) people in this way: "They [the women] collect the wild fruits and roots, attend to the horses or assist in that duty, cook, dress the skins and make all their apparel, collect wood and make their fires, arrange and form their lodges, and when they travel, pack the horses and take charge of all the baggage. In short, man does little else except attend his horses, hunt, and fish."

WHO'S WHO IN MONTANA?

Sacagawea (1784?–1812) was a Shoshone woman who served as a guide and interpreter for Lewis and Clark. She was the only woman traveling with the expedition. Today, the U.S. golden dollar bears her image in honor of her important role in this historic journey.

Lewis and Clark met a number of fur trappers, or mountain men, in Montana. John Colter, at first a member of the expedition, left the Corps to go fur trapping. Back at their starting point in St. Louis, Lewis and Clark reported that there were many fur-bearing animals in Montana.

As Jefferson had hoped, fur traders scrambled to get to Montana quickly. Manuel Lisa, a Louisiana Spaniard and director of the Missouri Fur Company, set off on a trading expedition up the Yellowstone River. In 1807, he established the first fur-trading post in Montana, at the mouth of the Big Horn River, called Lisa's Fort or Fort Manuel Lisa. In 1846, the American Fur Company built Fort Benton on the Missouri River. Today, Fort Benton is Montana's oldest permanent European settlement.

This sketch of a trout was done by Lewis and Clark during their expedition.

In the 1860s, steamboats on the Missouri River brought fur traders, gold seekers, and settlers to Fort Benton.

23

Fur trapping also drew mountain men to the Rockies, where they were befriended by local Native Americans. Jim Bridger, John Colter, and Jedediah Strong Smith were well-known mountain men who lived a rugged life in the mountains. They holed up in their cabins through the winter, and hunted in the spring and autumn. They traded horses, guns, and food with Native Americans in exchange for furs and buffalo skins. In summer, mountain men, Native Americans, and merchants often got together to trade furs and have a good time. Most mountain men spoke one or two Native American languages.

Eastern Iroquois people came to Montana with some of the fur traders. The Iroquois told the Salish about Christianity. In 1841, at the request of the Salish, Father Pierre-Jean De Smet founded St. Mary's Mission in the Bitterroot Valley. Father De Smet taught the Salish how to plant wheat and other food crops, and converted them to Roman Catholicism.

THE GOLD RUSH

In 1858, James and Granville Stuart discovered gold at Gold Creek. Not long after, gold was also discovered at Alder Gulch, about seventy-five miles (121 km) away, at Last Chance Gulch in Prickly Pear Valley, and at Grasshopper Creek in southwestern Montana. And so the Montana gold rush began.

During the five years of the gold rush, thousands of people poured into Montana. Miners set up camps wherever gold was discovered.

More than six hundred camps sprang up across Montana. Many camps grew into towns, and were sometimes referred to as "boom towns" because they grew so fast. Grasshopper Creek later became Bannack, Alder Gulch became Virginia City, and Last Chance Gulch was eventually renamed Helena.

The draw of gold brought immigrants from other countries, as well as people from across North America. Many people in the camps and towns spoke different languages. Most miners accepted people of different backgrounds; however, this was not true for Chinese or African-Americans. Chinese and African-Americans were usually forced to take the hardest and lowest-paying jobs. The Chinese often worked abandoned or worn-out mines or operated town laundries and restaurants. They were forced to live in separate parts of town. African-Americans, too, wound up working in low-paying jobs, such as laying railroad tracks or working as cooks.

Although many hard-working, honest people came to Montana, gold also attracted those who

These men are panning for gold in Montana.

hoped to get rich quick from the work of others. There was no effective law enforcement in the mining camps. Bandits attacked and killed miners on their way home from the mines. It was hard for the towns to keep law and order. Groups of citizens known as vigilantes tried to hunt down and punish criminals without the help of law enforcement. This didn't always work, however, and innocent people were sometimes killed.

In 1863 the Idaho Territory was formed, which included present-day Montana. The official territorial government was hundreds of miles away, separated by the Rocky Mountains. The huge distance made it difficult for the Idaho government to manage Montana effectively. In 1864, the United States government made Montana a separate territory of its own. After that, Montana became a safer and better place to live. Many miners brought their families to Montana. Schools and churches were built and theater groups were formed. On the Great Plains, land was also purchased for farming, which added to the state's economy.

Most mining towns didn't last long. When the gold ran out, they became ghost towns, or towns with very few residents. However, some mining towns became important communities. Missoula, Butte, and Helena were once mining towns. These towns prospered

EXTRA! EXTRA!

Many mining towns suffered from lawlessness. Virginia City's sheriff, Henry Plummer, was accused of secretly leading a band of thieves called "The Innocents," who killed more than one hundred people. In frustration, a group of outraged citizens from Bannack and Virginia City finally rounded up Plummer's band. In 1864, they caught Sheriff Plummer and hanged him—without a trial—on the gallows he himself had built.

Helena flourished as a mining town in the 1870s.

because they had many natural resources or were located on rivers that provided transportation to and from the area. For example, Butte became the copper mining center of the world long after most Montana gold mines were picked dry, and the large supply of lumber in Missoula helped it to become a center of the area's lumber industry.

WHAT'S IN A NAME?

Many names of places in Montana have interesting origins.

Name	Comes From or Means
Montana	Spanish or Latin word meaning "mountainous"
Absaroka Mountains	Original name of Crow Native Americans
Billings	Frederick Billings, president of the Northern Pacific Railroad
Bozeman	John Bozeman, who led the first wagon train into the Gallatin Valley
Kalispell	Kalispel Native Americans
Lewistown	Major William H. Lewis, who established Fort Lewis
Marias River	Named for Meriwether Lewis's cousin Maria Wood
Missoula	Probably a Salish word meaning "River of Awe" or "by the chilling waters"
Rocky Boy's Reservation	Misnamed for Native American chief Stone Child

NATIVE AMERICANS DEFEND THEIR LAND

Once Montana became a territory, changes occurred that threatened the lifestyle of Native Americans. Outsiders came to farm the land, build towns, and hunt buffalo and other game animals. Some of these new residents had no respect for the land or the people living there. Long before the gold rush, the United States government assigned specific lands, called reservations, to the Native American nations of Montana. For many years, miners, settlers, and even the United States government ignored the treaties (formal agreements) that created those reservations.

The Bozeman Trail created a special problem. Many settlers heading west traveled along well-marked trails, such as the Oregon Trail and the Mormon Trail. Near Montana, a new path called the Bozeman Trail split off from the Oregon Trail and headed toward Virginia City. It cut directly across Sioux hunting grounds, and the Sioux became increasingly hostile toward the white settlers. In 1865 and 1866, the United States government built forts Reno, Phil Kearney, and C.F. Smith to protect travelers along the Bozeman Trail.

A portion of the Bozeman Trail passed through an area (shown left) in southern Montana. The Bridger Mountains are in the background.

Throughout the 1870s, a series of battles occurred between Plains Indians and the United States Army. In 1876, the Sioux and Cheyenne joined together to battle the United States Cavalry. Smaller tribes, such as the Gros Ventres and Arapaho, banded together with the Sioux-Cheyenne force. The warriors were led by chiefs Sitting Bull, Crazy Horse, Rain-in-the-Face, Fast Bull, Crow King, and other proven war chiefs.

On June 25, 1876, Lieutenant Colonel George Armstrong Custer led 655 cavalry officers, troops, and scouts into the valley of Little Bighorn in southeastern Montana. Custer divided the regiment into three groups, with two smaller battalions sent along a different path. Custer's men galloped in rows toward what they thought was a defenseless Sioux village.

During the Battle of Little Bighorn, General George Custer and his men suffered a terrible defeat at the hands of the Cheyenne and Sioux.

As they approached, the main cavalry was surrounded by more than three thousand warriors. Of Custer's troops, only a scout survived. The Battle of Little Bighorn came to be called Custer's Last Stand.

One of the worst battles between Native Americans and the United States Army did not involve a local tribe, but one that was passing through the Montana territory. Like many other tribes, the Nez Perce also had treaties with the United States government that had been violated. They had lost not only their homeland in Oregon, but also a large reservation in Idaho. In 1877, Chief Joseph

EXTRA! EXTRA!

In reference to the Battle of Little Bighorn, the Sioux and Cheyenne called the cavalry "pony soldiers" because the troops rode horses. Infantry were given the name "walk-a-heaps" because they moved on foot. George Armstrong Custer was nicknamed "Yellow Hair" for his blond hair.

and the Nez Perce fled to Canada to escape being forced to live on yet another, smaller Idaho reservation. During their travels, the Nez Perce camped in Big Hole Valley, Montana, where the army ambushed them. For six days, the Nez Perce battled the cavalry as they continued to move north. They were finally stopped near Bears Paw Mountain.

This was the last major battle between Native Americans and the United States government. The Nez Perce lost six hundred of the roughly eight hundred in the band headed for Canada. Chief Joseph spoke to his warriors: "My heart is sick and sad. From where the sun now stands, I will fight no more forever."

By 1880, most of Montana's Native Americans had been moved to reservations throughout the territory. Many Native Americans died from European diseases like smallpox, chicken pox, and measles. What were once great herds of buffalo had now all been killed by hunters who boasted of slaying hundreds of beasts in one day. The focus of the Plains culture was gone.

Chief Joseph was the leader of the Nez Perce during the 1870s.

GROWING TOWARD STATEHOOD

The 1880s brought many changes in Montana. The Union Pacific Railroad was completed in Montana in 1881. The Northern Pacific Railroad crisscrossed the area by 1883. As transportation to the territory improved, the population of Montana steadily grew.

Montana became cattle country. Texas cowboys drove massive herds to Montana to graze on open land. The towns of Billings, Miles City, and Wibaux along the Northern Pacific line became rail stations from which cattle were shipped east.

Over time, however, the days of cattle drives and open grazing came to an end. Summer 1886 was one of the driest on record. Water supplies diminished and the cattle became weak. To make matters worse, the following winter was bitterly cold. Half to three-quarters of the cattle in Montana froze or starved to death. Many ranchers began to raise sheep because they were hardier. Farmers began to fence their croplands. These lands were off-limits to grazing cattle.

The population and the economy grew in the 1880s and 1890s. Overland trails and railroads provided a means for traveling to Montana, and people were drawn by its inexpensive farmland and mining opportunities.

Copper was discovered at Butte, and underground mining began. Thousands of immigrants came to Butte and nearby Anaconda for work. They came from other parts of the United States and from the British Isles, Central Europe, and Italy. Many were Irish or Cornish. Others were Jewish, African-American, and Chinese. Butte was a town that never slept. Miners worked around the clock, and businesses were open to serve them. As a result, Butte, which became known as "the richest hill on earth," grew into the biggest city in Montana.

William A. Clark and Marcus Daly, owners of the major copper mines, were known as the "Copper Kings." They grew extremely

wealthy and became rivals for power in Montana's businesses and government.

Eventually, Daly, Clark, and other mine owners sold their mining properties to a huge mining company called the Anaconda Company. Most Montanans called Anaconda simply "the Company." The Company grew so powerful that for years it controlled many other industries in Montana, including energy, logging, banking, publishing, and even the government.

By 1880, Montana had been a territory for sixteen years. Over the next ten years, the state's population grew from 39,000 to 143,000. In 1884, Montanans felt it was time to become a state. To do this, it needed a population of more than 60,000 and a state constitution.

Montana wrote two constitutions, and both were rejected by the United States government. The third constitution, written in 1889, was accepted.

Montana became the forty-first state on November 8, 1889. Joseph K. Toole became the first governor, and in 1894, Helena became the capital city.

THE EARLY TWENTIETH CENTURY

The early twentieth century was an exciting time in Montana. By 1909, several railroads crossed the state, including the Union Pacific, Northern Pacific, Great Northern, and Chicago, Milwaukee & St. Paul Railway (nicknamed Milwaukee Road). The railroad companies wanted farmers to settle along their routes. More farmers and farm products meant more business for the railroads.

Between 1900 and 1918, railroads, hometown newspapers, and chambers of commerce campaigned to bring farmers and other people into eastern Montana. Advertising campaigns were launched along the east coast, and brochures were sent to Europe. Thousands of homesteaders arrived. Some received 320 acres (130 hectares) of land under the United States government's Enlarged Homestead Act of 1909. Others bought land from the railroads or from individuals. By 1910, the number of farms in Montana had doubled and agriculture brought more money into the state than mining.

The state's population had also increased by half. Most homesteaders were native-born Americans, but many others were immigrants from Europe, especially from Germany and Scandinavia. Most were young, in their twenties and thirties, and a surprising number were single women. Many small towns grew to serve the needs of the new farmers.

In 1914, World War I (1914–1918) began. England, France, Russia, and Italy (the Allies) fought against Germany, Austria-Hungary, Bulgaria, and the Ottoman Empire (Turkey and parts of the Middle East). The United States did not enter the war until 1917, when the *Housatonic*, an American ship, was attacked and sunk.

The RICHEST ACRE of gold bearing ground in the world was found in the 60's in MONTANA. "WONDERLAND 1902" tells all about it. SEND SIX CENTS FOR IT TO CHAS. S. FEE, GEN. PASS. AGENT, ST. PAUL, MINN.

NORTHERN PACIFIC YELLOWSTONE PARK LINE

Advertisements such as this one attracted many newcomers to Montana.

Montana contributed a great deal to the war effort. Forty thousand soldiers from Montana fought in World War I. Also, the state's farmers produced additional crops to feed American soldiers. Farmers received good prices for their crops, and many farmers borrowed money to buy more land and more machines so they could increase production.

Meanwhile, in the mining industry, trouble erupted between labor (the miners) and management (the people who run the company). Miners' working conditions were dangerous and people often risked their lives to work in the mines. Many Butte miners were disabled or injured from falling rocks and explosions. After the Copper Kings sold their holdings to the Anaconda Company, conditions in the mines became even worse. Workers joined labor organizations called unions to help them fight for better and safer mining conditions, higher wages, and fewer work hours. Tension between the unions and mine owners gradually increased, and violence exploded twice in Butte—in 1914 and again in 1917. In August 1917, the federal government sent troops to occupy the city and to restore order. Although safety and other working conditions gradually improved, many other issues remained.

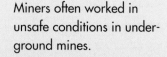
Miners often worked in unsafe conditions in underground mines.

At the same time, women were also fighting for their rights. In 1914, Montana women finally gained the right to vote in all elections. It wasn't until six years later, however, that the United States government passed an amendment to the Constitution giving all women the right to vote. In 1916, Montanans elected Jeannette Rankin to serve in the United States House of Representatives. She was the first woman to hold such a position.

DROUGHT AND DEPRESSION

Shortly after World War I, Montanans experienced difficult times. A terrible drought began in 1918, and this period of dryness affected many farms. In 1919, forest fires raced through the woodlands. Grasshoppers swarmed over the farmland. Crops were ruined and thousands of farms were abandoned. Between 1919 and 1925, half of all farmers in Montana lost their land because they could no longer afford to keep it. Many of Montana's banks failed. About sixty thousand people left the state, looking for work elsewhere.

The drought ended in the mid-1920s. However, bad times soon hit Montana—and the rest of the country—again. In October 1929, the New York Stock Market crashed. Many people around the country, as well as in Montana, had invested money in businesses through the stock market. When the value of those businesses decreased, so did people's investments.

The entire country fell into what became known as the Great Depression. People could no longer afford to buy things they needed, and as a result many companies couldn't sell their products. Fewer workers were needed, so thousands of people lost their jobs and many businesses closed.

Another drought hit Montana and other western states in the 1930s, continuing off and on for almost ten years. As the nation's economy slowed, demand for Montana farm products, lumber, and metals fell. The Montana state government did not have enough money to help its people.

In 1933, President Franklin Delano Roosevelt started the New Deal, a program to help end the Great Depression. To raise crop prices, the federal government paid Montana farmers to grow fewer crops. To create jobs, the Civilian Conservation Corps (CCC) was organized. This group hired people to fight forest fires, build public structures such as lookout stations and roads, and plant trees and grasses. In Montana,

fifty thousand workers built Fort Peck Dam on the Missouri River. It was one of the largest earth-filled dams in the world.

WORLD WAR II

In 1941, the United States entered World War II (1939–1945). The war helped pull America out of the Great Depression and put thousands of people back to work producing products that were needed for war.

Once again, Montana products were in demand. Meat, grains, and metals were all needed to help the Allies (France, England, Russia, and others) win the war against the Axis Powers (Germany, Austria, Italy, and Japan).

Montana both gained and lost population during the war. Thousands of people entered the state to take jobs in mining, lumbering, and farming. At the same time, thousands of others left the state for the Pacific Coast. They wanted higher-paying jobs, such as building ships and planes, than could be found in Montana.

During the war, some military installations were built in Montana. In 1942, a large Army Air Corps base, later called Malmstrom Air Force Base, was built near Great Falls. Also, the War Dog Training Center opened in Rimini. It served as a place to train sled dogs and men to rescue downed pilots in the Arctic regions. Communities around these bases grew because the bases needed support, such as restaurants, retail shops, and grocery stores.

THE LATE TWENTIETH CENTURY

Throughout the second half of the twentieth century, Montana's economy went up and down, mostly because the state relies heavily on natural resources and agriculture. Because the amount of rainfall varied from year to year, farmers and ranchers tried different varieties of crops and livestock. Cattle, wheat, and barley remained the state's most important agricultural products.

The start of open-pit mining in the 1950s brought the copper industry back to life. Open-pit mining is the process of digging up

In the 1950s, the Anaconda Company began open pit mining at Berkeley Pit in Butte.

blocks of earth and bringing them to the surface in order to remove minerals. Butte's first large-scale mine, called Berkeley Pit, opened in 1955. However, open-pit mining requires fewer workers, and jobs were lost. As a result, many people left Butte. Finally, in 1983, the Anaconda Company closed all mining operations in Montana. New methods for mining were eventually developed and are still used today, but the process is highly automated (worked by machines). Montanans are trying to make mining less destructive to the environment. Although mining still produces income for the state, it no longer provides high levels of employment.

FIND OUT MORE

Copper has long been an important natural resource for Montana. In what ways do we use copper in our daily lives?

Wood and paper products remained the major manufacturing industry in the late twentieth century. Montana also became a key producer of oil and gas during the 1970s. Coal production increased as well; much of the coal was used to produce electric power.

Aside from Montana's precious underground resources, one of its most important aboveground natural resources was threatened in the 1980s. In summer 1988, wildfires started by lightning strikes swept through Yellowstone National Park. The fires damaged hundreds of thousands of acres of forest and killed wildlife. Today, the areas that were badly affected by the fires are covered with grasses and wildflowers.

Fires raged in Yellowstone Park during the summer of 1988.

However, it will take generations for the majestic trees of Yellowstone to grow back.

In the 1990s, Montana became the focus of national interest. Certain groups of people who hold anti-government (against the government) beliefs have chosen to live in the area due to its isolation. One group that caught the attention of federal authorities was called the Freemen Movement. Its members were stockpiling weapons, refusing to pay taxes, and threatening to kill local authorities. In 1996, the FBI surrounded the group's compound in Jordan and tried to force them to surrender. The siege lasted eighty-one days, during which the group lived without outside contact other than the FBI. In the end, the group's leaders and many of its members were arrested.

EXTRA! EXTRA!

Although most forest fires are very destructive, some forest managers suggest that small, controlled forest fires may have long-term benefits. They help to clear the forest floor of pine needles, leaves, and fallen trees that have the potential to start a terrible fire under very dry conditions. Also, many large trees gain access to more sunlight, water, and nutrients after a forest fire has burned everything around them.

MONTANA IN THE TWENTY-FIRST CENTURY

Although Montana is still rich in natural resources, new advances in technology have led to fewer jobs in the state's traditional industries, such as farming, mining, and lumbering. As a result, Montana businesses and government are now working to diversify the economy. An organization called the Science and Technology Alliance is helping to find new ways to use Montana's natural resources. Other industries, such as manufacturing and tourism, are being expanded.

The environment is an important issue for today's Montanans. The state legislature has passed strong antipollution laws to address the damage that was done by strip mines and ore processing. Much of the forestland in Montana is publicly owned, and a number of citizen's groups are protesting lumbering in certain forests.

In 2000, Montana experienced major drought and many wildfires. In August that year, Governor Marc Racicot asked President Bill Clinton to declare the state a federal disaster area. Some people felt the fires were part of the normal drought cycle. Others, however, questioned the management of national forests and wondered if the fires could have been prevented. Finally, on the last day of August, the rains came.

Montana is also experiencing a water shortage as a result of the droughts. Because the land is so dry, there is a limited water supply in Montana. As more people move into the state, water rights issues are becoming more important, and towns and cities are all trying to stake a claim to certain amounts of water. Some towns have placed restrictions on water use, for example, making it against the law to water lawns. Water shortages are also causing special problems for the state's cattle ranchers. Hay and grass are in short supply due to the lack of water, and some ranchers are trucking cattle to far away pastures in an effort to find more grazing land. Some ranchers may even be forced to sell their cattle.

Through drought cycles and difficult economic times, Montanans continue to thrive. The story of the state is one of courage, survival, and appreciation for the beauty of the earth.

CHAPTER FOUR

GOVERNING MONTANA

When Montana became a state in 1889, it also adopted a constitution. The constitution lists the rights of citizens living in the state and the responsibilities of the government. Montana's first state constitution was ratified, or approved, in 1889.

Every twenty years Montana voters decide whether or not to hold a constitutional convention (a meeting) to review the constitution. Over time, people's needs and their view of government may change, creating a need for a change in the document. In 1972, a new constitution was written to replace the original. The updated constitution guarantees every person's right to privacy, and also makes a significant effort to protect Montana's environment.

Montana's constitution can also be altered by making amendments, or changes. An amendment may be proposed in one of three

The Montana capitol, built in 1902, is one of the most beautiful buildings in Helena.

ways: 1) approval by a majority of lawmakers, 2) a petition signed by Montana citizens, or 3) at a constitutional convention.

Montana's constitution is modeled after the United States Constitution. It divides the state government into three branches, or parts—executive, legislative, and judicial. Each branch is given specific responsibilities in order to keep the state running smoothly.

EXECUTIVE BRANCH

The executive branch is responsible for enforcing the state's laws. The governor is head of the executive branch. Montana governors serve four-year terms. While in office, he or she creates a budget for spending state money and also oversees the seventeen committees or departments that help run the state. The governor also has the power to veto (say "no") to new laws that are proposed by the legislature. The legislature is Montana's lawmaking body.

Other elected officials in the executive branch are the lieutenant governor, attorney general, auditor, secretary of state, and superintendent of public instruction. In the event the governor must give up his or her office, the lieutenant governor becomes governor. The attorney general is the link between the executive branch and the judicial branch, and represents the state in court trials. The auditor oversees the writing of a state budget, and the collecting and spending of state money. The superintendent of public instruction is in charge of state schools and the material taught in those schools.

MONTANA GOVERNORS

Name	Term	Name	Term
Joseph K. Toole	1889–1893	Sam C. Ford	1941–1948
John E. Rickards	1893–1897	John W. Bonner	1949–1952
Robert B. Smith	1897–1901	J. Hugo Aronson	1953–1960
Joseph K. Toole	1901–1908	Donald Nutter	1961–1962
Edwin L. Norris	1908–1913	Tim M. Babcock	1962–1968
Sam V. Stewart	1913–1921	Forrest H. Anderson	1969–1972
Joseph M. Dixon	1921–1925	Thomas L. Judge	1973–1980
John E. Erickson	1925–1933	Ted Schwinden	1981–1988
Frank H. Cooney	1933–1935	Stan Stephens	1989–1992
W. Elmer Holt	1935–1936	Marc Racicot	1993–2000
Roy E. Ayers	1937–1940	Judy Martz	2001–

Many state offices are located inside the capitol building.

LEGISLATIVE BRANCH

Montana's legislative branch makes state laws. These laws may cover everything from speed limits on state highways to laws protecting the environment. New laws that are proposed must be voted on and approved by a majority of the legislature before being sent to the governor for signing.

The Montana legislature is made up of two parts—the house of representatives and the senate. There are one hundred members in the house of representatives who serve two-year terms. There are fifty senators who serve four-year terms. Members of the house and the senate may not serve for more than eight years in a sixteen-year period.

JUDICIAL BRANCH

The judicial branch interprets the laws. Courts and judges make up the judicial branch. There are three levels of courts in Montana—city and municipal courts, district courts, and the Montana Supreme Court.

The first level of courts includes city and municipal courts. There are also justice of the peace courts and special courts, such as tribal courts and small claims courts, at this level. Many cases begin in these courts.

The second level is made up of district courts. District courts hear important criminal cases (cases where someone has broken a law) and civil cases (cases involving disputes between two parties who disagree on the meaning of a law). There are twenty district courts in Montana. The justices, or judges, of these courts serve six-year terms.

The highest court in Montana is the state supreme court. If a person is not satisfied with the outcome of their trial in a lower court, he or she may appeal to the supreme court, asking them to review the decision. The supreme court also supervises the lower courts. Six associate justices and one chief justice serve eight-year terms on this court.

TRIBAL GOVERNMENTS

There are seven Indian Reservations in Montana, including the Blackfeet Indian Reservation, Ft. Belknap Indian Reservation, Ft. Peck Indian Reservation, Rocky Boy's Indian Reservation, Northern Cheyenne Indian Reservation, the Crow Indian Reservation, and the Flathead Indian Reservation. Each reservation has its own tribal government in which tribal leaders are elected by majority vote of the adult membership. Each tribal government is responsible for lawmaking. In addition, each tribe sponsors celebrations and cultural activities, and promotes its language and unique heritage.

The Montana-Wyoming Tribal Leaders Council is an organization created by the member tribes to form a unified voice on common issues and concerns. The Council membership also includes the Northern

MONTANA STATE GOVERNMENT

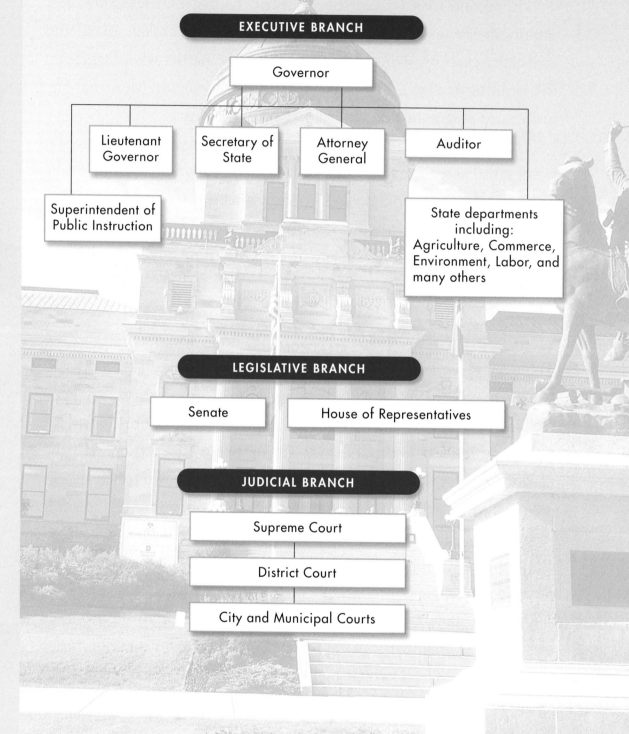

EXECUTIVE BRANCH

Governor

- Lieutenant Governor
- Secretary of State
- Attorney General
- Auditor

Superintendent of Public Instruction

State departments including: Agriculture, Commerce, Environment, Labor, and many others

LEGISLATIVE BRANCH

Senate   House of Representatives

JUDICIAL BRANCH

Supreme Court

District Court

City and Municipal Courts

Arapaho and Eastern Shoshone Tribes located on the Wind River Indian Reservation in Wyoming.

TAKE A TOUR OF HELENA, THE STATE CAPITAL

Helena is sometimes called "the gateway to the Rocky Mountains" because it is located along the eastern front of the Rockies. As capital cities go, Helena is small, with a population of 25,780. Despite its small population, the city is big on charm. The views are tremendous and the outdoor life is spectacular. Few residents would trade their small-town capital for big-city bustle.

The capitol building is a central point of the city. At the top of the building is a magnificent copper dome made from copper that was mined in Butte. Copper was chosen for the dome because of copper mining's tremendous influence on the state's economy. On top of the dome is a statue of

Nestled in the midst of several mountain ranges, Helena is often referred to as the "Queen City of the Rockies."

EXTRA! EXTRA!

Helena was originally named Last Chance Gulch. As the story goes, four miners had searched for gold in a number of places before camping in the Helena area. They decided this was their "last chance" to find gold before heading home to Georgia. The morning after making camp, they struck it rich! The town kept the name Last Chance Gulch until the 1860s, when it was renamed Helena, after a town in Minnesota. At first the name was pronounced HeLEENa. In 1882, locals changed the accented syllable, pronouncing the town name HELena.

Inside the chamber of Montana's house of representatives, Charles Russell's mural adorns the wall.

a woman in a long, flowing gown, called the Goddess of Liberty. She represents the freedom of Montana's people.

Inside the chambers of the house of representatives is a spectacular mural painted by Montana artist Charles M. Russell. The mural shows explorers Lewis and Clark asking the Flathead people about a safe route to the Pacific Ocean. The mural was painted in 1912.

Helena's many attractions will keep you outside in all seasons and in all types of weather. In the heart of the city lies Mount Helena City Park, which features nine hiking trails up Mount Helena. The trails vary in difficulty, but the view from the top is breathtaking. You can see all of Helena Valley and the surrounding mountains, and, with luck, soaring eagles and hawks.

Helena National Forest is home to bears, elk, moose, and countless birds. Inside the park are still more hiking trails. If you like wildflowers, you'll be richly rewarded in the Helena National Forest. Rare plants such as the calypso orchid, shooting star, Missoula phlox, cliff toothwort, and Klaus' bladderpod grow along the 700 miles (1,113 km) of forest trails.

In the center of town, take a walk down Last Chance Gulch, one of the city's main streets. It is named for the old mining camp from the 1800s.

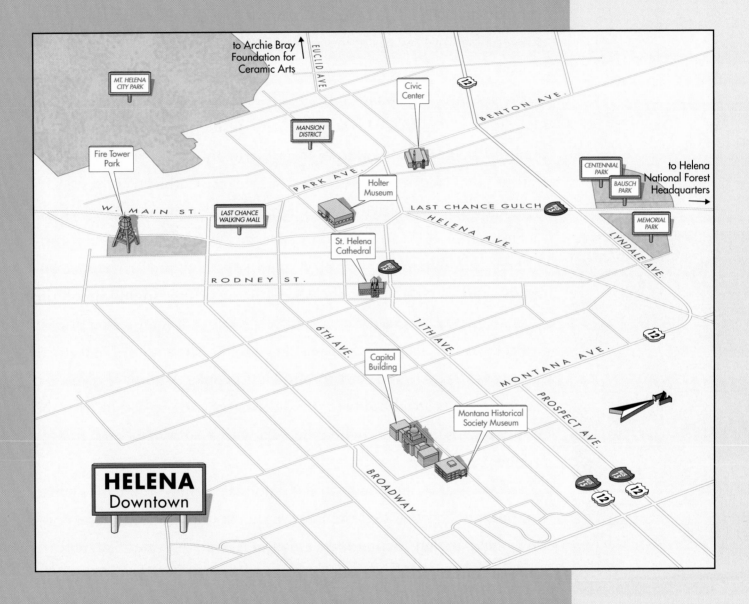

to Archie Bray
Foundation for
Ceramic Arts

EUCLID AVE.

MT. HELENA
CITY PARK

Civic
Center

BENTON AVE.

Fire Tower
Park

MANSION
DISTRICT

PARK AVE.

CENTENNIAL
PARK

to Helena
National Forest
Headquarters

Holter
Museum

BAUSCH
PARK

W. MAIN ST.

LAST CHANCE
WALKING MALL

LAST CHANCE GULCH

MEMORIAL
PARK

HELENA AVE.

LYNDALE AVE.

St. Helena
Cathedral

RODNEY ST.

6TH AVE.

11TH AVE.

Capitol
Building

MONTANA AVE.

Montana Historical
Society Museum

PROSPECT AVE.

BROADWAY

HELENA
Downtown

Pioneer Cabin, the oldest building in town, was built in 1865 during the Montana gold rush. The cabin has many of its original furnishings, so you can get a feel for how rustic life in the 1800s really was.

Not far from Last Chance Gulch is St. Helena Cathedral. This Roman Catholic church was built in 1924. The cathedral was designed to look like the cathedral in Cologne, Germany. Inside, the cathedral features beautiful stained-glass windows from Germany. While many churches feature saints and religious leaders, St. Helena Cathedral offers a surprise—the figures depicted in this church are of famous inventors!

Several museums are located in Helena. The Montana State Historical Society Museum displays more than two thousand artifacts, documents, and photos about the state's history. The highlight of the museum is the Mackay Gallery, which features a large collection of works by artist Charles M. Russell. The Holter Museum of Art features current works by regional artists and craftspeople. A number of Native American crafts are also shown. If you like to see art-in-action, visit the Archie Bray Foundation, where potter's wheels spin daily and artisans produce ceramic art.

Helena is also home to two major annual events—the Last Chance Community Powwow and the Race to the Sky sled dog race. The powwow, held in late September, celebrates Native American culture through music and dance. The sled dog race, held in winter, begins at Centennial Park in Helena and covers 350 miles (563 km) across the Continental Divide. Racers cross the rugged terrain multiple times, making it an extremely challenging—and especially exciting—race.

An artist spins a pottery wheel at the Archie Bray Foundation.

CHAPTER FIVE

THE PEOPLE AND PLACES OF MONTANA

In a sense, sprawling Montana is one gigantic neighborhood. It is made up of people who love the land, nature, and beauty that surround them. Although Montana is large in area, there are very few Montanans. In 2000, the population was 902,195; it ranked 44th in population among the states. In fact, in some Montana counties there are more than twice as many cattle as people!

The distribution of people in Montana is almost evenly divided between cities and rural areas. Fifty-three of every one hundred people live in cities, while the rest live on farms or in small towns. Even Montana's cities are small. Billings, the largest city, has a population of 89,847. Great Falls (56,690) and Missoula (57,053) are the next most populated cities. About one-third of Montana's residents live in the counties surrounding these three cities, as well as in Butte-Silver Bow, Bozeman, Helena, and Kalispell.

These children are wearing traditional dress of the Blackfeet Indian nation.

In Montana, ninety-one of every one hundred people are of European descent. Most of these people trace their ancestors to Germany, England, or Ireland. African-Americans and Asian Americans combined make up fewer than one person of every hundred, and two of every hundred people are Hispanic. Six in every hundred Montanans are Native American, making them the largest minority group in Montana.

Most of Montana's Native Americans live on reservations. There are eleven American Indian nations living on the state's seven reservations. Many Crow and Cheyenne live along the Wyoming border, in a reservation along the Little Big Horn River. The Blackfeet Reservation is in the north, along the border with Alberta, Canada. Others include the Fort Belknap, Fort Peck, Rocky Boy, and Flathead reservations. Among the tribes represented on the reservations are the Assiniboine, Atsina, Sioux,

EXTRA! EXTRA!

A small religious group called the Hutterites lives in southeastern and central Montana. The Hutterites came to Montana more than one hundred years ago. They live in small farming communities of about 120 people. The Hutterites follow traditional ways, much like the Amish and Mennonites. They worship daily, manage their finances and farms as a community, and run their own schools. For the most part, they do not use modern appliances, such as television sets or radios. A Hutterite community is called a *Bruderhof*. There are more than three hundred Bruderhof colonies in Montana, South Dakota, and Alberta, Canada.

Chippewa, Cheyenne, Gros Ventre, Pend d'Oreilles, Kootenai, Salish, Blackfeet, and Crow.

FIND OUT MORE

Population density is the average number of people in a unit of space. Montana has a low population density—for every square mile of land in Montana, there are only about six people (about two per square kilometer). In contrast, the state of New Jersey has about 1,135 people per square mile. How many people are in your classroom? Based on a rate of six people per square mile, about how many square miles would your class occupy if you all lived in Montana?

WORKING IN MONTANA

Most Montanans work in service jobs. People in the service industry perform some kind of work that other people or businesses need. Service workers include doctors, lawyers, teachers, real estate agents, and restaurant workers. About forty-four of every one hundred Montanans work in service industries. About twenty-two of every one hundred people work in wholesale or retail trades. These trades involve distributing products to stores and selling them to consumers.

Another important Montana industry is agriculture. Agriculture adds $2.3 billion to the state's economy each year. However, even though Montana's economy depends heavily on farming and ranching, most workers are not involved in agriculture. Only seventeen of every one hundred workers are employed in farming or ranching.

Montana's farms are larger today than they were fifty years ago, but they are fewer in number. There are about 59.9 million farm acres in Montana and 24,500 farms or ranches. The most important products are beef cattle, wheat, barley, and hay. Montana is second among all states in barley production. The state also produces alfalfa, cherries, and

A cowboy drives cattle in Montana.

57

sugar beets. Ranchers raise beef cattle, hogs, and sheep. There is a large dairy industry in the state as well.

In the past, mining was crucial to Montana's economy. Today, however, the influence of mining is not as strong. Petroleum and coal are mined to provide fuel for heat. Natural gas is also abundant in Montana and provides fuel for major cities and industries. Minerals such as copper, gold, lead, platinum, and zinc are all still mined in Montana. In fact, Montana is one of just three places in the world where platinum is mined. Today's mines are operated in large part by machines, which means that fewer people now work in mines than in the past.

Manufacturing is closely connected to the state's natural resources. The major manufactured products are lumber and wood products. The state's seventy sawmills turn out everything from pencils to board lumber to telephone poles. Other major manufacturing industries include food processing, paper making, and petroleum refining. Food-processing plants are located mainly in Great Falls and Billings, where most refining takes place as well.

To promote Montana businesses, the state government has created a "Made in Montana" label. This program, started in 1984, markets products that are made or produced in Montana. It is especially helpful to small businesses, which benefit from promotional materials and classes that are offered through the program. Some "Made in Montana" products include huckleberry soap, chokecherry jam, beef jerky, Native American jewelry, and western art.

Huckleberries grow in the mountainous regions of Montana, and only in the wild. They are used to make many delicious foods, including jam, jelly, and syrup, but they can also be used in products such as soap and candles. The easy recipe below makes mouth-watering huckleberry pudding.

EASY HUCKLEBERRY PUDDING
(serves 4)

4 slices bread
1 Tbsp. butter or margarine
2 cups huckleberries or blueberries
1/4 cup sugar or to taste
1/4 cup milk
Whipped cream or nondairy topping

1. Toast bread and butter it lightly.
2. Cut or tear buttered toast into small pieces. Place toast pieces in a bowl.
3. In another bowl, crush the berries.
4. Pour sugared berries over toast pieces.
5. Mix in milk.
6. Chill overnight. Serve with whipped cream or nondairy topping.

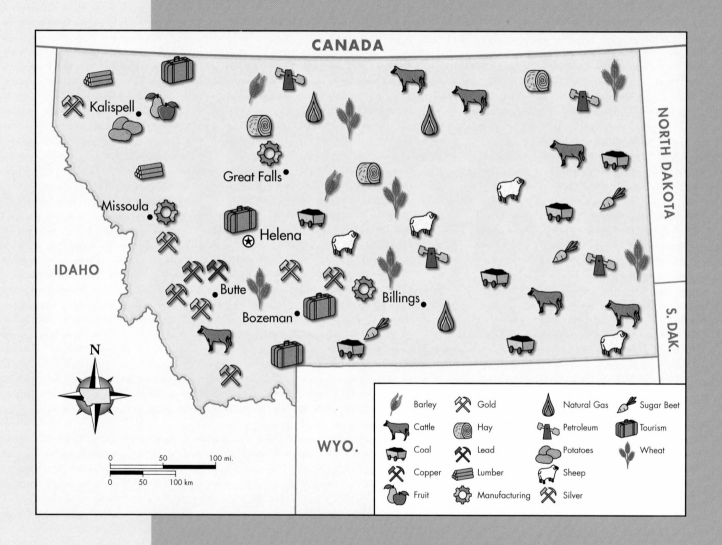

CANADA

NORTH DAKOTA

S. DAK.

IDAHO

WYO.

Kalispell

Great Falls

Missoula

Helena

Butte

Bozeman

Billings

N

0   50   100 mi.

0   50   100 km

Barley	Gold	Natural Gas	Sugar Beet
Cattle	Hay	Petroleum	Tourism
Coal	Lead	Potatoes	Wheat
Copper	Lumber	Sheep	
Fruit	Manufacturing	Silver	

An emerging industry in Montana is high technology, or businesses on the cutting edge of new and complex products. Aerospace industries, software designers, and manufacturers of computer parts are just a few of the businesses that are locating in Montana. For example, West Electronics makes circuit boards in Poplar, and S & K Electronics produces electronic parts in Ronan. In Helena, Summit Design and Manufacturing makes parts for use in airplanes and spacecraft.

Tourism is becoming increasingly important to the state. Tourism is the business of providing food, shelter, and entertainment for visitors. Today it is the second largest industry in Montana, bringing more than $1.5 billion in revenue. For people who love being outdoors, enjoy beautiful scenery, or delight in rugged wilderness adventures, Montana is the perfect vacation spot. Let's take our own tour of the state and see what Montana has to offer.

A hiker takes in the view at Glacier National Park.

TAKE A TOUR OF MONTANA

Western Montana

Let's start our tour in western Montana at Glacier National Park, located in the northern Rocky Mountains near the Canadian border. The park covers more than one million acres (404,686 ha) of mountain wilderness. Most people visit the park in summer,

A Blackfeet family gets ready for a powwow.

when wildlife is active, fishing is superb, and even high mountain passes can be reached if you put in the effort.

Glacier National Park is grizzly bear country. In late summer, you might observe grizzlies fishing for salmon in mountain streams. Stay clear! These bears are wild, and your family must keep a safe distance.

Near Glacier National Park are two Indian reservations. The Blackfeet Indian Reservation is at the park's eastern edge. Browning, a gateway town to the park, is the headquarters of the Blackfeet Nation. Every July, Browning hosts a four-day Native American celebration called North American Indian Days. Dance competitions, storytelling, and arts and crafts workshops are popular events.

The Flathead Indian Reservation is south of the park. It is home to the Salish and Kootenai nations. Part of the reservation is open to the public, and powwows are held in July in the villages of Arlee and Elmo. Tribal headquarters are at Pablo.

In 1908, President Theodore Roosevelt established the approximately 19,000-acre

(7,692-ha) National Bison Range on the Flathead Reservation. Roosevelt hoped to preserve the bison, sometimes called buffalo, which was in danger of extinction. At the time, there were only twenty wild bison left in the region. Today, up to five hundred bison live on the National Bison Range.

Our next stop is the city of Missoula, south of the Flathead reservation. Surrounded by mountains, the city is located near the point where three rivers come together—the Clark Fork, Bitterroot, and Blackfoot Rivers. Our first stop in the Missoula vicinity is the Lee Metcalf Refuge, which includes 2,800 acres (1,133 ha) of wetlands and woodlands dedicated to saving Montana wildlife. If you watch carefully, you'll see white-tailed deer drinking at ponds. Eagles and osprey soar across this region, where trumpeter swans, geese, and ducks make their summer nests. The *rat-a-tat-tat* you hear is a pileated woodpecker tapping the trees in search of a meal.

In Caras Park in Missoula, take a ride on the wooden carousel. Volunteer workers hand-carved the carousel's wooden horses. Not far from the carousel is the Missoula County Courthouse. On the inside of the courthouse walls is a series of murals painted by artist Edgar Paxon. The murals present a panoramic view of Montana's history as seen through the eyes of

Hundreds of bison graze on the National Bison Range near Flathead Lake.

FIND OUT MORE

Today, Berkeley Pit is filled with groundwater and rainwater. The water is polluted from heavy metals lining the sides of the pit. There is a danger that, in several years, this water will spill out. How could the overflow contaminate, or pollute, the land and other bodies of water around Butte? Find out what is currently being done to clean up the pit.

one of the West's most talented artists.

Southeast of Missoula is Butte. Butte is built on a steep hill among the remains of copper mines from the late 1800s. During that time, Butte produced more copper than any other place in the world. In the heart of town lies Berkeley Pit, which once operated as an open-pit mine. From 1955 to 1982, almost 1.5 million tons of copper were mined from it, leaving behind one of the biggest holes in the world. You can get a good look at the pit from the visitor's viewing stand.

Lewis and Clark Caverns State Park is a geological wonder east of Butte. These spectacular limestone caves are lined with stalactites (deposits of calcium carbonate that hang from the ceilings), and stalagmites (deposits that rise up from the ground), creating a moonlike landscape. Both formations

Stairs lead deep down into Lewis and Clark Caverns, where you can explore the limestone cave.

are made by slow-dripping water passing through limestone. These eerie underground rooms are still forming, as water continues to seep through the rock.

Our last stop in western Montana is Bannack, one of the state's most well-known ghost towns. In the late 1800s, it was a gold boomtown and for a brief time, capital of the Montana territory. Once the gold ran out it turned into an empty ghost town, where only the "ghosts" of past miners and townsfolk remained. Today, Bannack has been restored so that visitors can learn about Bannack's history and find out what life was like during the gold rush. Costumed actors play out stagecoach robberies, shootouts, and gold panning.

Central Montana

In west central Montana is the state capital, Helena. Directly south of Helena is Virginia City. In 1942, Sue and Charles Bovey visited Virginia City. At that time, many of the town's historic buildings were falling apart. The Boveys decided to save Virginia City and preserve it as a historic site. They

Virginia City was once a busy mining town.

bought the old buildings and restored them. To find out what an Old West town was really like, be sure to visit the general store, the local saloon, and the jailhouse.

Southeast of Virginia City is Yellowstone National Park. Most of the park lies in Wyoming, but the western entrance is in Montana. Yellowstone abounds with wildlife, including bears, elk, and bison. You'll also see geysers, bubbling mud pots, and smelly fumaroles, which are vents that emit steam smelling like rotten eggs.

Montana's Absaroka-Beartooth Wilderness is along the northern border of Yellowstone. This wilderness area includes two large national forests, one thousand lakes, and twenty-eight mountain peaks more than twelve thousand feet (3,658 m) high. They include Montana's highest mountain, Granite Peak (12,799 feet/3,904 m). Also, be sure to visit Grasshopper Glacier. Thousands of years ago, grasshoppers became frozen in the ice that covers the cliffs. Today, their remains are permanently fixed within the ice.

Two nearby sights are the Museum of the Rockies and Livingston, an historic Montana town. At the Museum of the Rockies, you'll learn about the dinosaurs that once roamed Montana's plains. Authentic art, clothing, and weapons of the Plains Indians and other Native American

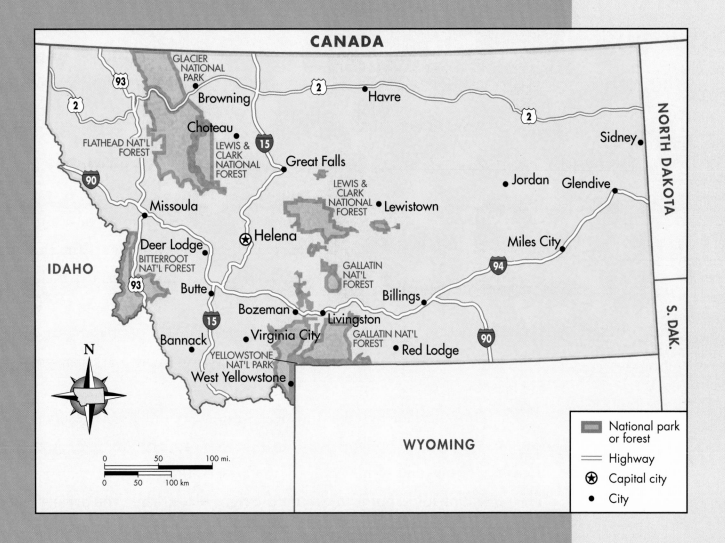

CANADA

GLACIER
NATIONAL
PARK

Browning

Choteau

LEWIS &
CLARK
NATIONAL
FOREST

FLATHEAD NAT'L
FOREST

Havre

Great Falls

LEWIS &
CLARK
NATIONAL
FOREST

Sidney

Jordan   Glendive

Lewistown

Missoula

Helena

Miles City

Deer Lodge

IDAHO

BITTERROOT
NAT'L FOREST

GALLATIN
NAT'L
FOREST

Butte

Billings

Bozeman

Livingston

Bannack

Virginia City

GALLATIN NAT'L
FOREST

Red Lodge

YELLOWSTONE
NAT'L PARK

West Yellowstone

NORTH DAKOTA

S. DAK.

WYOMING

N

0   50   100 mi.

0   50   100 km

National park
or forest

Highway

Capital city

City

tribes are also on display. In Livingston's downtown historic district, you can walk down the same streets that Martha "Calamity Jane" Canary once did. Buildings on Main Street look much as they did when Calamity Jane lived in town.

Located in south central Montana, Billings is the state's largest city. It was founded in 1877 as a trading post and stage station. The Montana Fair, the largest statewide annual event, is held every summer at MetraPark and Yellowstone Exhibition Grounds in Billings. There are pie-baking and jam-making contests, livestock exhibits, and amusement park rides at the fair.

The Crow Indian Reservation, near Billings, is the largest reservation in Montana. The land is beautiful, rich, and productive. Arapooish, a Crow, said of his land, "The Crow country is good country. The Great Spirit has put it in exactly the right place; while you are in it you fare well; whenever you go out of it, whichever way you travel, you fare worse."

The reservation has farm and grazing land, a coal mine, and a buffalo herd of about three hundred. The annual Crow Fair is held at Crow Agency each August. The Crow people celebrate their heritage through parades, dance competitions, arts and crafts, and traditional foods. Chief Plenty Coups State Park, named for the last of the great Crow chiefs, is located on the Crow reservation.

In north central Montana, visit the C.M. Russell Museum Complex. Charles Russell was an Old West artist who lived in Great Falls. People from all over the world attend a yearly auction at the museum, which contains the world's largest collection of his art.

Eastern Montana

In eastern Montana you'll find the mysterious badlands. The many canyons and strange rock formations of the badlands were carved by water erosion. Near Glendive, Makoshika State Park is one badlands area in which the ridges, valleys, and cliffs are particularly beautiful. Many dinosaur fossils have been found in this area.

North of Culbertson is Medicine Lake National Wildlife Refuge. Lakes, ponds, and marshes cover almost half the refuge. The refuge is home to a large white pelican colony. Other birds that nest in the area include many varieties of ducks, geese, whooping cranes, and egrets. For a good view, you can climb up a 100-foot (31-m) viewing tower.

FIND OUT MORE

Fossils are the remains of ancient animals and plants that have been preserved in the earth's crust. How are fossils formed? How long does it take for a fossil to form?

MONTANA ALMANAC

Statehood date and number: November 8, 1889, forty-first state

State seal: The current seal is similar to an earlier seal created in 1864. It features mountains, the Great Falls, mining and farming tools, and the state motto: *Oro y Plata*. Adopted 1893.

State flag: The Montana state flag has a dark blue background with the word Montana across the top. A picture of the original great seal is in the center. Adopted 1905.

Geographic center: Fergus, 8 miles (13 km) west of Lewistown

Total area/rank: 147,046 square miles (380,849 sq km)/ 4th

Borders: Idaho, Wyoming, South Dakota, North Dakota, Canada

Latitude and longitude: Approximately between 44° 23' and 49°N and 104° 02' and 116° 02'W

Highest/lowest elevation: Granite Peak, 12,799 feet (3,901 m) above sea level/Kootenai River, 1,800 feet (549 m) above sea level

Hottest/coldest temperature: 117°F (47°C) at Glendive on July 20, 1893 (also at Medicine Lake, July 5, 1937)/–70°F (–57°C) at Rogers Pass on January 20, 1954

Land area/rank: 145,556 square miles (376,990 sq km)/4th

Inland water area/rank: 1,490 square miles (3,859 sq km)/15th

Population/rank (2000 census): 902,195/44th

Population of largest cities:

  Billings: 89,847

  Missoula: 57,053

  Great Falls: 56,690

  Butte: 33,892

  Bozeman: 27,509

  Helena: 25,780

Origin of state name: From Spanish *montana*, meaning "mountainous"

State capital: Helena

Counties: 56

State government: 50 senators, 100 representatives

Major rivers/lakes: Missouri, Yellowstone, Jefferson, Madison, Milk, Gallatin, Bighorn, Little Bighorn, Tongue, Powder, Kootenai, Teton, Marias, Sun, Bitterroot, Flathead, Clark Fork, Musselshell Rivers/Flathead Lake, Fort Peck Lake, Hungry Horse Reservoir, Canyon Ferry Reservoir, Lake Koocanusa (partly in Canada)

Farm products: Wheat, barley, dairy products, cherries, sugar beets, hay, hogs, and honey

Livestock: Cattle and calves, sheep and lambs

Manufactured products: Food products, wood and paper products, printing and publishing, petroleum and coal products

Mining products: Copper, gold, Portland cement, platinum, lead, and zinc

Animal: Grizzly bear

Ballad: "Montana Melody," words by LeGrande and Carleen Harvey, music by LeGrande Harvey. Adopted 1983.

Bird: Western meadowlark

Fish: Blackspotted cutthroat trout

Flower: Bitterroot

Fossil: Maiasaura (duck-billed dinosaur)

Gemstones: Sapphire and moss agate

Grass: Bluebunch wheatgrass

Insect: Mourning Cloak butterfly

Motto: *Oro y Plata* ("Gold and Silver," in Spanish)

Nicknames: Treasure State, Big Sky Country

Song: "Montana," words by Charles C. Cohan, music by Joseph E. Howard. Adopted 1945.

Tree: Ponderosa pine

TIME**LINE**

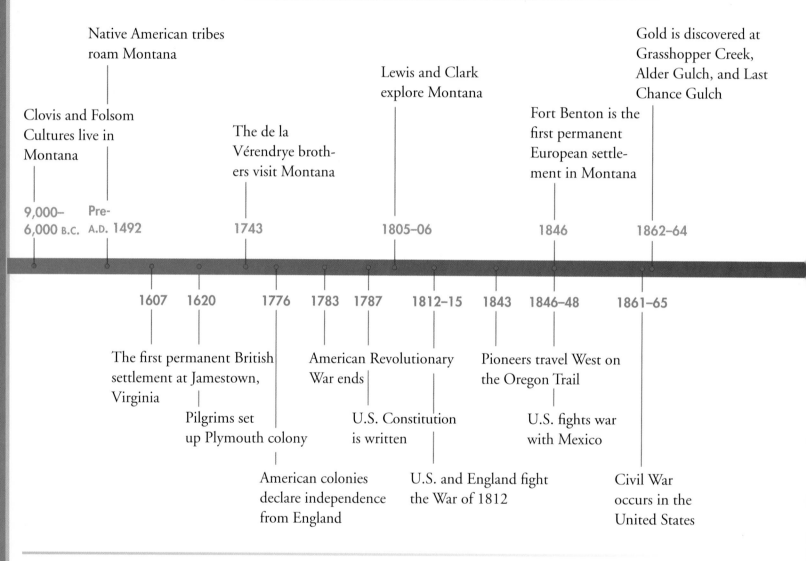

Native American tribes
roam Montana

Gold is discovered at
Grasshopper Creek,
Alder Gulch, and Last
Chance Gulch

Clovis and Folsom
Cultures live in
Montana

Lewis and Clark
explore Montana

Fort Benton is the
first permanent
European settle-
ment in Montana

The de la
Vérendrye broth-
ers visit Montana

| 9,000–6,000 B.C. | Pre-A.D. 1492 | 1743 | 1805–06 | 1846 | 1862–64 |

| 1607 | 1620 | 1776 | 1783 | 1787 | 1812–15 | 1843 | 1846–48 | 1861–65 |

The first permanent British
settlement at Jamestown,
Virginia

American Revolutionary
War ends

Pioneers travel West on
the Oregon Trail

Pilgrims set
up Plymouth colony

U.S. Constitution
is written

U.S. fights war
with Mexico

American colonies
declare independence
from England

U.S. and England fight
the War of 1812

Civil War
occurs in the
United States

UNITED STATES **HISTORY**

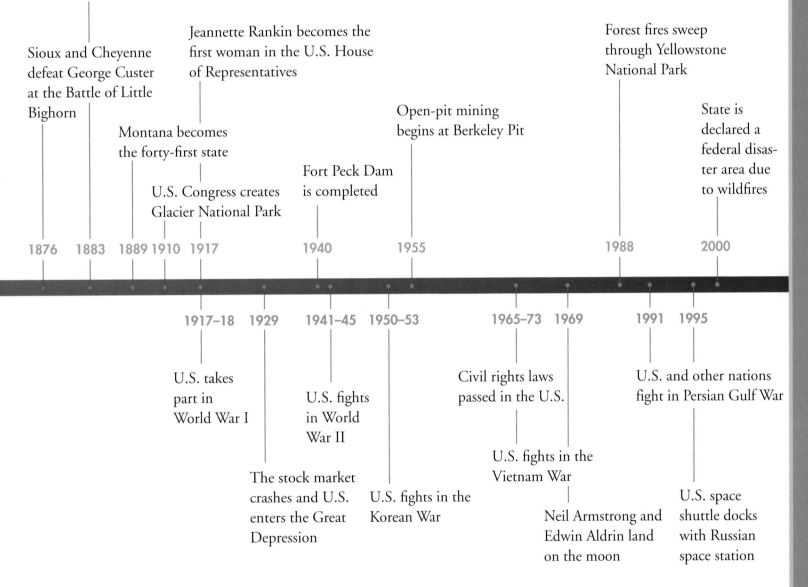

Northern Pacific Railway connects
Montana to the coasts

Jeannette Rankin becomes the
first woman in the U.S. House
of Representatives

Forest fires sweep
through Yellowstone
National Park

Sioux and Cheyenne
defeat George Custer
at the Battle of Little
Bighorn

Open-pit mining
begins at Berkeley Pit

State is
declared a
federal disas-
ter area due
to wildfires

Montana becomes
the forty-first state

Fort Peck Dam
is completed

U.S. Congress creates
Glacier National Park

1876 1883 1889 1910 1917   1940   1955   1988   2000

1917–18 1929   1941–45 1950–53   1965–73 1969   1991 1995

U.S. takes
part in
World War I

Civil rights laws
passed in the U.S.

U.S. and other nations
fight in Persian Gulf War

U.S. fights
in World
War II

U.S. fights in the
Vietnam War

The stock market
crashes and U.S.
enters the Great
Depression

U.S. fights in the
Korean War

Neil Armstrong and
Edwin Aldrin land
on the moon

U.S. space
shuttle docks
with Russian
space station

GALLERY OF FAMOUS MONTANANS

Eric Bergoust
(1960–)
Freestyle skier. He was the winner of the 1998 Olympic Gold Medal in Men's Aerials and winner of the 1999 World Freestyle Championship in Switzerland. Born in Missoula.

Alice Greenough
(1902–1995)
First woman named to the Cowgirl Hall of Fame and the National Cowboy Hall of Fame. Born in Red Lodge.

A.B. Guthrie, Jr.
(1901–1991)
Writer of Western novels. *The Big Sky*, about mountain men in Montana, is his most famous book. He won a Pulitzer Prize for *The Way West*, about life on the Oregon Trail.

John R. Horner
(1946–)
Paleontologist who has discovered many dinosaur fossils in northcentral Montana, including the first almost whole dinosaur egg in the Western Hemisphere. He is the Curator of Paleontology at the Museum of the Rockies in Bozeman and has served as an adviser on the films *Jurassic Park* and *The Lost World*. Born in Shelby.

Dorothy M. Johnson
(1905–1984)
Writer of Western novels and short stories, as well as books for children. Lived in Missoula.

Wallace D. McRae
(1936–)
Rancher and award-winning cowboy poet. Spokesperson for Montana arts and the environment. He lives in Forsyth.

Robert Edward (Ted) Turner, III
(1938–)
Media and sports executive, philanthropist. Owner of the Atlanta Braves, a major league baseball team. Turner owns several ranches in Montana, where he keeps endangered animals.

James Welch
(1940–)
Writer of poems, novels, and nonfiction, mostly about the Blackfeet people. He was born in Browning and raised on the Fort Belknap Reservation. He lives in Missoula.

GLOSSARY

butte: isolated hill or mountain with steep sides

capital: city or town where the seat of government is located

capitol: building where governing bodies meet

climate: general weather conditions of a particular place over a long period of time

constitution: basic set of laws of a state, nation, or other political unit or organization

convention: group of people or organizations assembled for a common purpose

diversify: to introduce variety

drought: dry period, especially when crops do not grow or are damaged

economy: system of producing and distributing goods

extinction: no longer existing due to a dying out of the species

fossils: remains of ancient plants and animals trapped in rock

geothermal: hot water and steam that is used to produce energy

glacier: large body of slow-moving ice

hydroelectric: water power that is used to produce electricity

paleontologist: scientist who studies fossil remains of plant and animal life

pishkun: buffalo jump

prehistoric: the time before written history

reservation: land that is set aside by formal agreement for the use of Native Americans

rural: relating to the country

technology: scientific or modern ways of doing work

turbine: engine that is activated by pressure from water, steam, or gas

FOR MORE INFORMATION

Web sites

Montana Online

http://www.discoveringmontana.com/css/default.asp
Official Web site for the Montana state government.
You can access government agencies here, state news-
papers, and cities or towns.

Montana Kids

http://www.montanakids.com
http://kids.state.mt.us
State of Montana Web site for kids. Sections include
Montana's Past, Agriculture and Business, Things to
See and Do, Plants and Animals, Montana Facts,
Features, and Activities and Games.

Montana

http://visitmt.com/
A Web site that offers tourist information.

Books

Hoyt-Goldsmith, Diane. *Buffalo Days.* New York, NY:
Holiday House, 1997.

Patent, Dorothy Hinshaw. *Where the Bald Eagles
Gather.* New York, NY: Clarion Books, 1990.

Shirley, Gayle Corbett. *Four-Legged Legends of Montana.*
Helena, MT: TwoDot, 1993.

Stein, R. Conrad. *Cornerstones of Freedom: Lewis and
Clark.* Danbury, CT: Children's Press, 1997.

Addresses

Montana Historical Society
P.O. Box 201201
225 North Roberts
Helena, MT 59620-1201

Montana Chamber of Commerce
2030 11th Avenue
Helena, MT 59624

The Governor of Montana
State Capitol
Helena, MT 59620-0801

INDEX

MEET THE AUTHOR

Judith M. Williams grew up in Wisconsin. In high school, Williams traveled to Montana by train. Ever since, she has had a special interest in Montana. Williams graduated from St. Olaf College in Northfield, Minnesota, and attended Columbia Teachers College in New York City. After working in the publishing field for many years, she became a freelance writer. She researched this book using the Internet, the telephone, and the library.

Photographs © 2002: AP/Wide World Photos: 39 (Montana Historical Society), 49; Archie Bray Foundation for the Ceramic Arts/Roger Mathis: 54; Archive Photos/Getty Images: 27; Brown Brothers: 36; Carl and Ann Purcell: 15, 16, 61, 70 right; Chief Plenty Coups State Park: 68; Chuck Haney: 13; Corbis-Bettmann: 74 bottom left (James L. Amos), 64 bottom (Macduff Everton), 74 bottom right (Douglas Kirkland), 37, 42 (UPI); Dave G. Houser/HouserStock, Inc.: 65 (Jan Butchofsky-Houser); David R. Frazier: 41, 45, 50; Dembinsky Photo Assoc./Stan Osolinski: 71 right; Denver Public Library, Western History Collection/Colorado Historical Society, Denver Art Museum: 25; H. Armstrong Roberts, Inc.: 4 (T. Dietrich); Hulton Archive/Getty Images: 22 (by Charles Russell, Amon Carter Museum) 17, 30, 31, 66; Lynn M. Stone: 63; MapQuest.com, Inc.: 70 bottom left; Montana Historical Society, Helena: 34, 70 top left; National Cowgirl Museum and Hall of Fame, Fort Worth, TX: Network Aspen/Nicholas DeVore III: 12 bottom; 74 top left; North Wind Picture Archives: 8, 18, 23 bottom, 23 top, 29, 35; Photo Researchers, NY: 69 (James L. Amos), 20 (Tom McHugh), 51 (Joe Sohm/Chromosohm), 3, 9 (Jim Steinberg), 12 top (Art Wolfe); Robert Holmes Photography/Dewitt Jones: 56; Stock Montage, Inc.: 33; Stone/Getty Images: 7 (Glen Allison), 57 (Steve Bly), 3, 10, 55, 62 (Paul Chesley), 71 left (Darrell Gulin), cover (Art Wolfe); University of Montana, Missoula, MT: 74 top right (96-105, Collection, K. Ross Toole Archives); Visuals Unlimited: 64 top (David S. Addison), 48 (Mark E. Gibson), 52 (L. Linkhart)